B♭ BASS CL

M000026635

ACCENT ON ACHIEVEMENT

John
O'Reilly
and
Mark
Williams

The "Keys" to Success: Progressive Technical & Rhythmic Studies in all 12 Major and 12 Minor Keys

Dear Band Student:

Congratulations on completing the first two books of
ACCENT ON ACHIEVEMENT. Book 3 will help you to develop
the musical and technical skills necessary for a lifetime of great
music-making. Your "Keys" to success include scales,
exercises and fun tunes in all 12 major and 12 minor keys.
You'll learn new rhythms and meters, and also improve your
tone and intonation while playing a rich variety of chorales.
With diligent practice, there's no end to what you can accomplish!
We wish you the best in your quest for musical excellence.

John O'Reilly   Mark Williams

Instrument photos (cover and page 1) are courtesy of Yamaha Corporation of America.

Alfred

ACCENT ON CONCERT Bb MAJOR

CHORALE: CHILDREN'S PRAYER from "HANSEL AND GRETEL"

Engelbert Humperdinck
(1854–1921)

C MAJOR SCALE (CONCERT Bb)

INTERVAL WORKOUT

SCALE STUDY

CHROMATIC SCALE

ACCENT ON RHYTHM: 9/8 Time

MORNING HAS BROKEN

Irish Folk Song

ACCENT ON RHYTHM: 12/8 Time

ANDANTE CANTABILE from "SYMPHONY NO. 5"

Peter I. Tchaikovsky
(1840–1893)

ACCENT ON CONCERT G MINOR

CHORALE: BASED ON A THEME BY NEUMARK

Johann Sebastian Bach
(1685–1750)

Andante

A MELODIC MINOR SCALE (CONCERT G)

INTERVAL WORKOUT

SCALE STUDY

A HARMONIC MINOR SCALE (CONCERT G)

ACCENT ON RHYTHM: 3/2 Time

15

Count: 1 & 2 & 3 (e) & a

RONDO

Henry Purcell
(1659–1695)

Maestoso

16

f

Fine

mf   *p*   *mf*

D. C. al Fine

THE WILD HORSEMAN

Robert Schumann
(1810–1856)

Allegro

17

mf

Fine

mp

D. C. al Fine

ACCENT ON CONCERT Eb MAJOR

CHORALE: BE THOU MY VISION

Traditional Irish Melody

F MAJOR SCALE (CONCERT Eb)

INTERVAL WORKOUT

SCALE STUDY

CHROMATIC SCALE

ACCENT ON RHYTHM: ♫·

Count: 1 & 2 & 1 e(&a)2 &

THE KEEL ROW

English/Scottish Folk Song

Allegretto

mf

f

ACCENT ON RHYTHM: ♪♪♪♩ and ♪♪♪♪♪♪

Count: 1 e (&) a 2 & 1 & a (2) e &

PETITE OISEAU

Traditional

Moderato

mp

mf

ACCENT ON CONCERT C MINOR

CHORALE: PRELUDE IN C MINOR

Frèdèric Chopin
(1810–1849)

ACCENT ON RHYTHM:

THREE WAYS TO SWING IT

ACCENT ON RHYTHM: *Swing Eighth Notes*

THE BATTLE OF JERICHO

American Spiritual

ACCENT ON CONCERT F MAJOR

CHORALE: SINE NOMINE

Ralph Vaughan Williams
(1872–1958)

36 Maestoso

G MAJOR SCALE (CONCERT F)

37

INTERVAL WORKOUT

38

SCALE STUDY

39

CHROMATIC SCALE

40

ACCENT ON RHYTHM: ♫ in 6/8 Time

41

Count: 1   2 & 3   4 & 5   6

THE IRISH WASHERWOMAN

Traditional

Allegro

42

LIP SLUR/FLEXIBILITY STUDY

43

ACCENT ON CONCERT D MINOR

CHORALE: PICARDY

17th Century French Melody

E MELODIC MINOR SCALE (CONCERT D)

INTERVAL WORKOUT

SCALE STUDY

E HARMONIC MINOR SCALE (CONCERT D)

ACCENT ON RHYTHM: ♪. ♪♪ in 6/8 Time

GREENSLEEVES

English Folk Song

ACCENT ON RHYTHM: ⅟ (Sixteenth Rest)

LA CUMPARSITA

G. Matos Rodriguez
(1897–1948)

ACCENT ON CONCERT A♭ MAJOR

CHORALE: HOW FIRM A FOUNDATION

Early American Melody

Moderato

53 *mf* *mp* *mf* *rit.*

B♭ MAJOR SCALE (CONCERT A♭)

54

*See Fingering Chart on page 38.

INTERVAL WORKOUT

55

SCALE STUDY

56

CHROMATIC SCALE

57

*See Fingering Chart on page 38.

ACCENT ON RHYTHM: 5/4 and 6/4 Time

PROMENADE from "PICTURES AT AN EXHIBITION"

Modest Mussorgsky
(1839–1881)

WALTZ from "SYMPHONY No. 6"

Peter I. Tchaikovsky
(1840–1893)

ACCENT ON CONCERT F MINOR

CHORALE: THE GOD OF ABRAHAM PRAISE

Hebrew Folk Song

61 Moderato

G MELODIC MINOR SCALE (CONCERT F)

62

INTERVAL WORKOUT

63

SCALE STUDY

64

G HARMONIC MINOR SCALE (CONCERT F)

65

ACCENT ON RHYTHM:

Think: 1 2 3 4 5 6   1 2 3 4 5 6

SOMETIMES I FEEL LIKE A MOTHERLESS CHILD

American Spiritual

TRIPLET TUNE

ACCENT ON CONCERT C MAJOR

CHORALE: IT IS WELL

Phillip Bliss
(1838–1876)

D MAJOR SCALE (CONCERT C)

INTERVAL WORKOUT

SCALE STUDY

CHROMATIC SCALE

ACCENT ON RHYTHM: *Changing Meters* — $\frac{2}{4}$ through $\frac{6}{4}$

Count: 1 & 2 & 3 & 4 &   1 & 2 & 3 &

SOLILOQUY

Andante

LIP SLUR/FLEXIBILITY STUDY

Accent on Concert A Minor

Chorale: Based on a Theme by Hassler

Johann Sebastian Bach
(1685–1750)

ACCENT ON RHYTHM:

PRELUDE from "**L'A**RLESIENNE"

Georges Bizet
(1838–1875)

CAPRICE **N**O. 24

Nicolo Paganini
(1782–1840)

ACCENT ON CONCERT Db MAJOR

CHORALE: LONDONDERRY AIR

Irish Folk Song

85 Andante

Eb MAJOR SCALE (CONCERT Db)

86

*See Fingering Chart on page 38.

INTERVAL WORKOUT

87

SCALE STUDY

88

CHROMATIC SCALE

89

ACCENT ON RHYTHM: Changing Meters — 6/8 and 2/4

WASSAIL SONG

Traditional Carol

ACCENT ON RHYTHM: Changing Meters — 6/8 and 3/4

FIESTA MARIACHI

ACCENT ON CONCERT B♭ MINOR

CHORALE: KOMM, SÜSSER TOD

Johann Sebastian Bach
(1685–1750)

C MELODIC MINOR SCALE (CONCERT B♭)

INTERVAL WORKOUT

SCALE STUDY

C HARMONIC MINOR SCALE (CONCERT B♭)

Accent on Rhythm: ⅝ Time

Count: 1 2 3 4 5

Fun With Five

Accent on Rhythm: Changing Meters with ⅜ , ⅝

Variations on a Star Song

Count: 1 2 3 4 5 6 7

ACCENT ON CONCERT G MAJOR

A MAJOR SCALE (CONCERT G)

103

INTERVAL WORKOUT

104

CHROMATIC SCALE

105

LA CUCARACHA

Mexican Folk Song

106 Allegretto

AULD LANG SYNE

Scottish Folk Song

107 Andante

ACCENT ON CONCERT E MINOR

F# MELODIC MINOR SCALE (CONCERT E)

INTERVAL WORKOUT

F# HARMONIC MINOR SCALE (CONCERT E)

LA CINQUANTAINE

J. Gabriel-Marie
(1852–1928)

Allegretto

*A*CCENT ON CONCERT G♭ MAJOR

A♭ MAJOR SCALE (CONCERT G♭)

112

INTERVAL WORKOUT

113

CHROMATIC SCALE

114

MICHAEL, ROW THE BOAT ASHORE

American Spiritual

115 Andante

mp

MARCH OF THE MEN OF HARLECH

Welsh Folk Song

116 Moderato

f

ACCENT ON CONCERT E♭ MINOR

F MELODIC MINOR SCALE (CONCERT E♭)

117

INTERVAL WORKOUT

118

F HARMONIC MINOR SCALE (CONCERT E♭)

119

THEME from "SWAN LAKE"

Peter I. Tchaikovsky
(1840–1893)

120

ACCENT ON CONCERT D MAJOR

E MAJOR SCALE (CONCERT D)

121

INTERVAL WORKOUT

122

CHROMATIC SCALE

123

ALLELUIA

17th Century Melody

124 Moderato

SHENANDOAH

American Folk Song

125 Adagio

ACCENT ON CONCERT B MINOR

C♯ MELODIC MINOR SCALE (CONCERT B)

126

INTERVAL WORKOUT

127

C♯ HARMONIC MINOR SCALE (CONCERT B)

128

HATIKVAH

Israeli National Anthem

Maestoso

129

ACCENT ON CONCERT A MAJOR

B MAJOR SCALE (CONCERT A)

130

INTERVAL WORKOUT

131

CHROMATIC SCALE

132

BINGO

American Folk Song

133

MY BONNIE LIES OVER THE OCEAN

Traditional

134

ACCENT ON CONCERT F♯/G♭ MINOR

G♯ MELODIC MINOR SCALE (CONCERT F♯)

135

*Double-sharp: Raises the pitch of a note two half steps. (F double-sharp = G natural)

INTERVAL WORKOUT

136

G♯ HARMONIC MINOR SCALE (CONCERT F♯)

137

THEME from "SCHEHERAZADE"

Nicolai Rimsky-Korsakov
(1844–1908)

Moderato

138

Accent on Concert C♭ Major

D♭ Major Scale (Concert C♭)

139

Interval Workout

140

Chromatic Scale

141

The Bluebells of Scotland

Scottish Folk Song

Moderato

142

mf

f

mf

Beautiful Dreamer

Stephen Foster
(1826–1864)

Andantino

143

mp

1.

2.

mf *mp*

rit. *p*

ACCENT ON CONCERT A♭ MINOR

B♭ MELODIC MINOR SCALE (CONCERT A♭)

INTERVAL WORKOUT

B♭ HARMONIC MINOR SCALE (CONCERT A♭)

HAVA NAGILA

Hebrew Folk Song

ACCENT ON CONCERT E MAJOR

F# MAJOR SCALE (CONCERT E)

INTERVAL WORKOUT

CHROMATIC SCALE

HOME ON THE RANGE

Moderato

American Folk Song

ACCENT ON CONCERT C♯/D♭ MINOR

E♭ MELODIC MINOR SCALE (CONCERT D♭)

152

INTERVAL WORKOUT

153

E♭ HARMONIC MINOR SCALE (CONCERT D♭)

154

WE THREE KINGS

Traditional Carol

155 Moderato
mp

BASS CLARINET FINGERING CHART

HOME PRACTICE RECORD

Week	Date	ASSIGNMENT	Mon	Tue	Wed	Thur	Fri	Sat	Sun	Total	Parent Signature
1											
2											
3											
4											
5											
6											
7											
8											
9											
10											
11											
12											
13											
14											
15											
16											
17											
18											
19											
20											
21											
22											
23											
24											
25											
26											
27											
28											
29											
30											
31											
32											
33											
34											
35											
36											